Children and Communion

Communion

A Practical Guide for Interested Churches

Peter Reiss

Assistant Curate, St Martin's, Sherwood

GROVE BOOKS LIMITED
RIDLEY HALL RD CAMBRIDGE CB3 9HU

Contents

Acknowledgements

My thanks to the clergy of North Nottingham Deanery and in Nottingham.
To Howard Worsley, Steve Pearce and Ian Bunting for their help, advice and comments.
To Gilly Myers and Jeremy Fletcher and the Grove Worship Group.
To St Martin's, Sherwood, for their friendship and tolerance.
To Neil Burgess for letting me take on the project.
To Rex Elson for the cover design.

The Cover Illustration is by Rex Elson, redrawn for publication by Peter Ashton

First Impression October 1998
ISSN 0144-1728
ISBN 1 85174 385 5

1
Introduction

If only...if only Jesus had left clear instructions and guidelines, life would be so much easier. Instead of just having a final meal at Passover time with his disciples, Jesus could have left detailed instructions on how to remember it and how to do it, and who could participate and how. Instead we have developed various traditions and patterns, and have often become very partisan and protective towards them, quite unaware of the developments within our own tradition and the variety of practice through time and in different places. This is certainly true with regards the practice of baptized infants and children receiving communion.

In Bohemia in the 1400s, in the Hussite communities, children were welcome to receive communion.[1] In the Orthodox and Oriental traditions children have received communion from baptism, as indeed was the case in the early Middle Ages in Europe. Now, in the 1990s, the Church of England, along with other Anglican Provinces and with other denominations, is struggling with the issue of admitting baptized children to communion, going at different paces in different places, too fast for some and not fast enough for others. There is confusion, hurt, variant practice and as yet no clear pattern.

In the church where I am the curate, for several years now and with the bishop's support, children have received communion, from about the age of eight and after instruction. The catalyst for this, in part, was a family whose child was already a communicant member of another tradition. Charlotte, as a communicant member of that church was welcome to receive communion at St Martin's, but her friends were not. This anomaly needed to be addressed. Other churches also will find themselves challenged by similar situations to deal with the reasons for including or excluding children from communion. Many churches want to address the issue, but do not know where to start.

This booklet is an attempt to look at the issue of children receiving communion prior to confirmation, the objections people have, the new Bishops' Guidelines, the implications and the practicalities. It is not comprehensive by any means, and happily acknowledges and builds on the previous Grove Books on the subject, in particular the theological justification for baptized children being admitted to communion.[2] It takes a deliberately 'contextual' focus, recognizing that church practice is influenced by social circumstances and culture, and not simply derived from 'pure theology.'

1 See D Holeton, *Infant Communion—Then and Now* (Grove Liturgical Study No 27, Nottingham: Grove Books, 1981).
2 C Buchanan, *Children in Communion* (Grove Worship Series No 112, Nottingham: Grove Books, 1990). Also D Young, *Welcoming Children to Communion* (Grove Worship Series No 85, Nottingham: Grove Books, 1983).

The issues and questions that I tackle come from discussions and research with many clergy and congregations in the Nottingham area, those who have admitted children, those in the process of doing so, and those who do not. I have surveyed many of the Nottingham Anglican churches—the more 'Catholic' and the more 'Protestant,' inner-city, city centre, suburban, estate, and small town. Some have many children most Sundays, some very few. I have also discussed the issues with ministers from other churches.

Until recently in the Church of England all children were excluded from communion, and few raised a voice on their behalf; communion, like some films, carried a 12 certificate, not a 'U' for Universal. It was generally understood that one waited to be confirmed, though the practice has grown of children going to the rail for a blessing, and, in some churches, even receiving sweets at the rail. The House of Bishops staved off any real discussion of the practice, despite national and international statements affirming the right of all the baptized to partake in the communion. Some parents have surreptitiously given a fragment of their bread to their children. People are anxious to know what is proper and right. They are also anxious about the implications for their worship on a Sunday if children share communion regularly. For some, simply the feeling that they are doing something very new makes them nervous.

There needs to be informed discussion, a chance to think together, to listen, and to move forward. I hope this booklet can help in that process. The booklet is designed to be practical and contains study questions so that it can be used as the focus for group discussions if that is helpful.

2

The Theological Issues Surrounding the Debate and the Context of Today

What we may claim to believe and what actually happens of a Sunday can be two very different things. While we may claim a unity within our denomination, in fact there are many and variant theologies and priorities being expressed. The Church of England, and to a lesser extent the Methodist Church, is broad enough to contain the more Catholic (with an emphasis on gathering for the Sacrament), the more Protestant (with an emphasis on gathering under the Word preached), and the more Pentecostal (with an emphasis on gathering in the presence of the Spirit). In most churches, because of the building and local history ('the previous vicar did this!'/'we've always done it like this') there are local peculiarities.

We cannot consider the place of children at communion properly until we have acknowledged our particular context, and the place and understanding of communion, and of baptism, in our own church. This is not simply a matter of 'churchmanship'; it means knowing what matters for the congregation, and they may have very different ideas from the minister!

- What do people think that they are *doing* when they take communion, celebrate the eucharist, or remember the Lord's Supper in *your* church?[3]

The Sacraments are Signs of Belonging as Well as Marks of Belief

Our understanding of membership of the church, of the requirements for joining or for belonging, and of how one does join, will, necessarily, be affected by, and affect our understanding of the church. Today we have the twin problems of those who say they believe, but do not wish to belong to a church, and those who wish to belong, but may have less than orthodox beliefs. It is recognized that 'belonging' often precedes 'believing' for many people now.[4] This means that we will want to help people belong, to feel included, as a pathway to faith. Through history, the church has struggled with where baptism fits on a person's journey into faith and discipleship. Three extremes are the rejection of sacraments (Quakers and Salvation Army), Christendom (where all children should be baptized), and the Baptist model (where baptism is reserved for those who have made a coherent profession of faith). Though the meaning of baptism is disputed, it is generally agreed that only the baptized should take communion,[5] and that the baptized should take communion regularly.[6]

In the Church of England the reality is that most of the baptized do not take communion at all frequently, simply because they are not in church. There are around 25 million baptized 'members,' but only about one million communicants of a Sunday. Even those who have been confirmed are mostly 'absent members,' but regular attenders, children, who are baptized, are currently excluded from the family meal. Whatever we think, we need to work with this reality.

Within the reality of our context we need to decide the role and place of the sacraments in our church life. Is baptism the beginning, middle or end of an exploratory or joining process? What else is rightfully a part of that process

---

3 The questions in this chapter are foundational but also very broad. They are important for the issue of children receiving communion, but they also raise a host of other issues too. If they are being used in a group discussion, the leader(s) will need to be vigilant!

4 John Finney's recent research gives empirical evidence of this in *Finding Faith Today* (Bible Society/Churches Together in England, 1992).

5 It must be said that this is Baptist theology, but in practice, in many Baptist churches and other independent churches, children are included in communion services—the logic being, it seems, that baptism is a sign of mature commitment, not of church membership.

6 Whether quarterly for a Presbyterian or weekly for an Anglican or Roman Catholic.

of initiation, and when is it appropriate for the person to take communion? Might confirmation be described as a further step towards belonging, and so a fit entry to communion? That is how it has been seen in practice (since the Victorian period),[7] but it is hard to justify such a process from the Bible.[8]

- What do the two sacraments actually signify to people today? (Probably not what we intend them to signify!)
- How do you feel about other traditions that treat the sacraments very differently?
- Can you find strengths in their patterns and systems, for example, in the daily Mass of the Catholic culture or the quarterly communion of the Presbyterian culture?
- Is there a question concerning sporadic attenders and their *right* to receive communion if communion is a sign of belonging?

Baptism and Communion Go Together
The baptizing of infants is justified on the understanding that baptism is to do with grace, and that the child is to be brought up within the family of the church. In exactly the same way adults are baptized, as a sign of God's grace, and so they may belong to the family of God. There is one baptism, whether the person is an infant or a centenarian, and it is done to us, however able we might be. Accepting this line of thinking (and of course Baptists and others rather emphasize the person's conscious decision), then it is not only illogical but virtually a form of excommunication to deny the family member the family meal. If the baptism of infants is valid, then those infants must be welcome to receive communion. As baptism is the sign and seal of our 'beginning to belong,' our entry into the family of God, so the eucharist, the Mass or the partaking in the memorial meal is the sign of our 'being in belonging,' that we are members of the family of God, the body of Christ, the fellowship of believers. Recent Anglican and WCC statements have all affirmed that baptism is the sufficient as well as necessary sacrament of access.

'In the celebration of the eucharist, all the baptized are called to participate in the great sign of our common identity as the people of God, the body of Christ, and the community of the Holy Spirit.'[9]

---

7 See C Buchanan, *Anglican Confirmation* (Grove Liturgical Study No 48, Nottingham: Grove Books, 1986).
8 In passing we should recognize the historical shifts of emphasis with baptism, from an immediate sign (*eg* Lydia, or the Philippian jailer—Acts 16) to the end of a lengthy catechumenate process in the 4th century.
9 Principle 1 of the Principles and Recommendations of the Fifth International Anglican Liturgical Consultation, Dublin 1995; in D Holeton (ed), *Renewing the Anglican Eucharist* (Grove Worship Series No 135, Cambridge: Grove Books, 1996).

But deep down many Anglicans (especially the more evangelical) are not happy with infant baptism and feel it is only made respectable by the later confirmation by the candidate of his or her beliefs. The baptized infant is, it seems, in an intermediate position of membership, and thus can be denied the right of receiving the second sacrament.[10]

- What is your gut response to the statement: 'All baptized (including the very young) are welcome at the Lord's Table'?
- In some churches an 'Agape Meal' is shared, involving bread and wine, and at which children (and the non-baptized) can be present and share. Can we distinguish between such a 'Fellowship Meal' and a communion service? Are both valid?[11]

Social Forces, Theological Argument

Society have always put pressure on the churches; the churches have always been conditioned to a greater or lesser extent, consciously and subconsciously, by the world and surrounding cultures. Today it is no different. Belonging is an 'in' word; as church numbers fall, we want to be as inclusive as possible. Where children were excluded from adult things a century ago and less, now the move is to include them wherever possible; witness, for instance, the explosion in 'Family Pubs.' The language we use, the (in)formality of our services, the variety we offer (for we live in a supermarket culture), all these are now choices we must make and assess. Are we changing our views and practice because of the social pressure to include children (or resisting because of the social pressure from older people to keep to tradition) or are we able to make this a theologically focused issue, where we do what we do for good theological reasons?

- What pressures exist in our church, whether to change and include, or to maintain?
- From where and from whom do they come?

---

10 This is what some call the Mason-Dix Line, after the two significant theologians who taught such a view. It is in effect a two-tier view of membership.
11 I raise this, because it is a real problem in some churches and strikes at the heart of the desire to include others in our worship.

3
Why a Reluctance to Admit
Children to Communion?

The common reasons given to exclude children, particularly the youngest children, from communion can be divided into four categories.

The Educational Argument

'But young children don't understand...' And nor do we...fully! Faith is about learning, and grace is about being given something. That is why we come to church, and why we bring our children. We do not presume, and nor do they. They understand a gift, and they understand what is special, and, like us, their attitude and behaviour varies. Colin Buchanan addresses more fully the issue of understanding/discernment in a previous Grove booklet[12]; I would prefer to highlight the contextual history of this argument.

In passing we have noted that in the early church children did receive communion; this was a practice that was changed for various reasons. In the Reformation it was not an issue; what was an issue was defending 'truth,' and the enemies were on both wings, Puritan/Baptist and Rome. In this climate it is no surprise that the BCP, following on from the 1549 and 1552 *Prayer Books* made confirmation (confirmation being dependent on knowledge of the Catechism) the entry to communion. Interestingly the Presbyterians also made understanding and right practice a prerequisite when they held power in the 1640s. Having abolished the *Book of Common Prayer* they imposed a 'Directory of Public Worship.' An Act of Parliament in 1644 gave presbyters the right to exclude any who could not give sufficient understanding of the faith, as well as those who lives were not sufficiently good or godly. The result, as Holeton puts it, was 'a rather self-satisfied Puritan bourgeoisie.'[13]

The admission of children was much debated in the seventeenth century, but for polemical not pastoral reasons. Those opposed to infant baptism argued that paedobaptists were illogical to exclude the baptized from the other sacrament. Some paedobaptists did accept the admission of infants to communion in principle, but did not pursue it. Jeremy Taylor concluded that 'the communion of infants was lawful, but not necessary, and that for the peace of

---

12 *Children in Communion* (pp 10–12). He deals specifically and well with the 'problem verses' 1 Corinthians 11.28–29: 'Examine yourselves, and only then eat of the bread and drink of the cup. For all who eat and drink without discerning the body, eat and drink judgment against themselves' (NRSV).

13 D Holeton, *Infant Communion—Then and Now*, p 17. Also C Buchanan, *Anglican Confirmation*, pp 28–29,44,47–48.

the church at that time, the question could be left at that.'[14]

Through the eighteenth and nineteenth centuries the Church of England changed in its structures and its practices—as, of course, did society—but the issue of including children in the communion was not raised. The eighteenth century majored on 'submission' of women, children and servants under God[15]—this did not promote the equality of all at God's table! The Victorian era saw a huge restructuring of the church, with new movements and practices, and a new professionalization,[16] or rather a new understanding of the clerical profession,[17] including the promotion of episcopal confirmation.[18] What was new then is now considered 'traditional,' whether Christmas trees and cards, or confirmation practice or organs and robed choirs. Since then confirmation has been justified as part of a two-stage initiation model, by Dix and Archbishop Geoffrey Fisher in particular, and only now are church leaders emerging who did not learn under this 'two-stages of initiation' school.

But we should also note the continuing influence of this view—the necessity for 'understanding' prior to receiving. The Bishops' Guidelines (see next chapter) require prior preparation of the child, and the 'minimum age,' though not specified, seems to have been set according to an educational theory that considers the age of 6/7 to be an age when many children develop a new stage of understanding, one suitable for understanding communion. There are those who support children receiving communion from 6/7 years old, but strongly object to the baptized infant receiving. They justify this by claiming 6/7 years old is an age of sufficient understanding.

It must be made very clear that those who support the inclusion of all the baptized at communion do not in any way dismiss the need for instruction or for understanding. What they stand against is the requirement that instruction precedes reception, as if instruction is necessary as well as baptism. All Christians as part of their discipleship should always be 'learners,' clergy included. The eucharist is a meal for the road, not for the homecoming—that meal is the heavenly banquet!

Although I reject the argument that instruction is needed prior to reception,

---

14 D Holeton, 'Communion of All the Baptized and Anglican Tradition' p 30, in Ruth Meyers (ed), *Children at the Table* (New York: The Church Hymnal Corporation, 1995). Jeremy Taylor's work was highly influential; Holeton's essay is an excellent summary of a little known debate. His view is that the paedobaptists were hard put to defend their existing position but knew a more radical change of practice would have been too divisive.

15 See S Gill, *Women and the Church of England* (London: SPCK, 1994) Chapter 1 for a good general discussion on the potency of this doctrine in the 19th century.

16 See A Russell, *The Clerical Profession* (London: SPCK, 1980).

17 Rosemary O'Day challenges Russell's thesis, saying it was the Reformation that changed the clergy from an 'Estate' to a profession. Subsequently this 'professionalism' was worked out and changed; she does not deny the great changes to the church in the Victorian era. 'The Clerical Renaissance in Victorian England and Wales,' pp 184–212 in G Parsons (ed), *Religion in Victorian Britain* (Manchester: Manchester University Press, 1988).

18 For the first time bishops got around their dioceses and confirmation actually happened. Bishops were not going to allow unconfirmed children to take communion when they were working hard to promote the importance of confirmation.

because it is so frequent it needs to be dealt with thoroughly. *Theologically*, it is hard to defend infant baptism while opposing the baptized infant's place at the communion table. If baptism does not require prior understanding, then why does communion? If the sacraments are to do with grace, then let the children who belong partake. *Historically*, there is simply not enough evidence in the earliest churches to convince either way, and all practice necessarily has a contextual element. *Developmentally*, we need to recognize the limits of educational theory. While it may be true that children do develop conceptually around the age of 6/7, this *conceptual* development may not be a *spiritual* development. Spiritual development is not the same as educational development. The sense of wonder, of mystery, of awe present in many very young children needs kindling and nurturing. Young children know what a gift is and learn good practice by copying. Purely from a pragmatic perspective, it may be that instilling reverent practice in a 3/4 year old is easier than in a 6/7 year old.[19] And of course as will be mentioned later, any age limit is so obviously arbitrary and unjustifiable theologically that it is bound to cause trouble.

The Ritual Argument

At one meeting I attended where the subject of children and communion was being discussed, a woman put her objection like this: 'When we give a dinner party and get out the best china, we don't want the children there; it's just not suitable. It's a time for adults, the children have their own types of party suitable for them.' Young children crying, laughing, running, complaining will spoil the beauty of the service, will not appreciate the order and solemnity of the activity. Like an adult film, the eucharist should carry a 15 sign, or at least a PG, parental guidance. Why should everything be reduced to the lowest common denominator for accessibility?

Who, though, is on the guest list for communion? And, who, for that matter, is the host? Whether we are more Catholic or more Protestant, the presence of children as full communicant members of our churches will raise serious questions about our ritual. There is a rich heritage in our liturgy and practice, and it need not be scrapped, but something has gone terribly wrong if we prefer good ritual or whatever before making other baptized Christians welcome and included. But those who have less of a ritualistic background need to recognize the added 'discomfort' the admission of children to communion will bring to such churches. (The 'ritual' may, however, simply be the need for quiet and reverence in the service, not the trappings of anglo-catholicism, which may well be far more interesting and visual to a small child than the bareness and 'word'-centredness of a more low church tradition). Those

---

19 Fritz Oser has done quite a bit of work on spiritual development in children, and his research would favour the inclusion of children younger than 6 purely for developmental reasons.

of a more Protestant background may need to assess the cerebral nature of their faith; to love God with heart and soul as well as mind is part of the great Commandment.

If children are separated for the word, can they also not be separated for the sacrament? They could have their tea in the nursery! Surely not if the sacrament is a sacrament of belonging, of family unity and of grace. The sacrament *must* be accessible to all the family, and ritual must be subordinate to that, however that is then worked out. This does not exclude having services geared more to adults *on occasion*, or services geared more to children if appropriate.

The Emotional/Psychological Argument

These are the most important and the least important issues in the debate. They are least important because they are subjective, can only be defended with much blustering, and have no clear biblical warrant. And for the same reason they are the most important, because they are held despite good theological or scriptural backing. They may emanate from the shadow-side of those whose faith requires human supports, is weak and stained with the world; they may be sub-culturally conditioned fleshly responses to a movement of the Spirit, but who said we should denigrate the feelings of our brothers and sisters in Christ? We may have been given the opportunity to study further, and have taken it, *we* may feel we can see clearly, but for many others, whose faith is precious, albeit unsure, the continued changes in church practice are unsettling. 'Here they go with yet more changes,' is the feeling.

'Why can't they wait, as we had to, till confirmation?'
'If you feel that strongly, then confirm them at 7.'
'Children will misbehave and make light of something precious.'

Many have been brought up with a prayer book unchanged for centuries, and with church practice that did not seem to have changed substantially for years, and was already out-of-step with modern moods, and good for just that reason. They have been taught that God does not change, that we are to hold firm to what we have been taught, that there is a deposit of faith. They feel that Christian Britain is becoming progressively more modern/secular/pagan/immoral and so forth. For them, moves that seem to pander to modern trends—such as the inclusion of children and the dumbing down of 'culture'— are immediately suspect, in the same way that those who see God as the God of the future, who grew up with themes like 'development' and 'progress' as buzzwords, will rush to embrace new and less formal ideas.

It is as important to 'hear' the unspoken emotions as it is to listen to articulated theologies. If common sense is the philosophy of the people (Gramsci), then 'It feels wrong' can be the stoutest defence against those who argue brilliantly for new ideas. Are we aware of where we draw *our* lines, of what feels

11

wrong to us? We may be happy to see children receive communion, but what about them helping with the administration and distribution of the elements? Feeling uncomfortable about something is not comfortable.

Practical Issues

There are a number of practical objections made to children receiving communion.

1. *Infants will spill or dribble, can't manage a cup or will leave crumbs.*

Until the late 13th century very young children were communicated in one kind, the wine. The minister can easily put a drop on a baby's lips, and even have a somewhat diluted chalice for youngsters. If we can sort out the practicalities of administration at old people's homes and in hospitals, we can work them out in churches, though we may have to rethink what forms the distribution can take.

2. *Children who have been out at 'Sunday School' have been absent for the confession, and find the Eucharistic Prayer boring. If they are full members should they not be present for the full service?*

There are in fact two issues here, one of involvement and one of the suitability of the service for younger people. If the children have been 'out' in groups, that does not mean that they have not been a part of the worshipping community, and if current liturgies are inappropriate then we need alternatives that are better. The group leaders can surely help prepare the children to be ready when they come back to the main congregation, whatever point of the service that is. Family meals should not be dominated by 'adult-talk.'

3. *What about visiting children, who are not baptized?*

There is the feeling that visiting children will copy their communicating friends. If the church has a practice of offering a blessing then the child can receive a blessing, just as a non-communicating adult might. Do we, as adults, forgo receiving because our friends are not baptized or communicant? Behind this question is the bigger issue of belonging, believing and becoming addressed in the previous chapter. It is actually about how we welcome anyone, not just children, and it hints at possible double standards.

4. *What of the unbaptized children of church members?*

This is a more difficult pastoral issue. It relates to children who are regular members but, for good reasons, have not been baptized, probably because of a 'Baptist' theology held by parents, or at least no convinced theology of infant baptism. While we might wish to include them, we should ask what church traditions would include them. From conversations with local ministers of different traditions in Nottingham the answer is not clear. A local Methodist is very inclusive, welcoming everyone in practice, while a local Baptist and a local Independent, while recognizing that children do sometimes take the bread and wine as it comes round, would want to see the youngster baptized before being a regular communicant, the Baptist accepting 10 as the lowest normal age for baptism, the Independent putting 14/15 as the lowest. Infant baptism for church members has more force if it is paired with taking communion.

- Which of these arguments are 'strong' in your church, and/or in your own mind?
- Are you convinced that baptism is the beginning of membership of the church?
- Can you honestly separate the genuine objection from an unwillingness to allow change?
- If the psychological/emotional objections are strong, how might they be addressed?
- How do we best help those who feel uncomfortable with what is happening?
- Do you know how adults who are not taking communion feel in your church?
- Do you know how the children feel? Could you find out? Might this help?
- Is it reasonable to expect that a service can really work well for infant, child, teenager and adult all together?

4

The Bishops' Guidelines

These are the Guidelines agreed by the House of Bishops early in 1997, with regard to 'The Admission of Baptized Persons to Holy Communion before Confirmation.'

The Text

a) Since 'communion before confirmation' is a departure from our inherited norm, it requires special permission. After consultation, every diocesan bishop will have the discretion to make a general policy whether or not to entertain new applications for 'communion before confirmation' to take place in his diocese. If he decides to do so, individual parishes must seek his agreement before introducing it. The bishop should satisfy himself that both the incumbent and the Parochial Church Council support any application, and that where appropriate ecumenical partners have been consulted. If the parties cannot agree, the bishop's direction shall be followed.

b) The incumbent must ensure that the policy adopted for his/her parish is clearly and widely understood. The policy should be considered within the general context both of the ministry that is carried out in the parish through initiation, and also of the continuing nurture of people in the Christian faith. The bishop should be satisfied that the programme of continuing Christian nurture is in place leading to confirmation in due course.

c) Before admitting a person to communion, the priest must seek evidence of baptism. Baptism always precedes admission to Holy Communion.

d) There is a question regarding the age at which children may be admitted to Holy Communion. In general the time of the first receiving should be determined not so much by the child's chronological age as by his or her appreciation of the significance of the sacrament. Subject to the bishop's direction, it is appropriate for the decision to be made by the parish priest after consultation with the parents, or those who are responsible for the child's formation, with the parents' goodwill. An appropriate and serious pattern of preparation should be followed. The priest and parents share in continuing to educate the child in the significance of Holy Communion so that (s)he gains in understanding with increasing maturity.

e) The Church needs to encourage awareness of many different levels of understanding, and support the inclusion of those with learning difficulties in the Christian community. Particular care needs to be taken with the preparation of any who have learning difficulties, including children. The incumbent should consult with those concerned in their care, education and support regarding questions of their discernment of the sacrament, their admission to Communion, and their preparation for confirmation.

14

f) Before a person is first brought to Holy Communion, the significance of the occasion should be first explained to him/her and to his/her parents, and marked in some suitable way before the whole congregation. Wherever possible, the person's family should be involved in the service.

g) A register should be kept of every person admitted to Holy Communion before confirmation, and each should be given a certificate (or, better, the baptismal certificate should be endorsed).

h) Whether or not a parish practises 'communion before confirmation', the incumbent should take care regarding the quality of teaching material, especially that used with children and young people. The material should be reviewed regularly and the advice of diocesan officers and other professional advisers taken into account.

i) The priest must decide exactly how much of the liturgy communicant children will attend. Even if there is a separate 'Ministry of the Word' for children, anyone who is to receive Holy Communion should be present in the main assembly at least for the eucharistic prayer.

j) No baptized person, child or adult, who has once been admitted to Holy Communion and remains in good standing with the church, should be anywhere deprived of it. When, for example, a family moves to another area, the incumbent of the parish they are leaving should contact their new incumbent to ensure that there is no confusion regarding the communicant status of children. It is the responsibility of the new incumbent to discuss with the children and parents concerned when the children should be presented for confirmation. Such children should normally be presented at least by the age of 18.

k) Since baptism is at the heart of initiation, it is important for the bishop regularly to be the minister of holy baptism, and particularly at services where candidates will be both baptized and confirmed. It is generally inappropriate for candidates who are preparing for initiation into the Christian life in baptism and confirmation to receive baptism at a service other than the one in which they are to be confirmed.

l) In using rites of public reaffirmation of faith other than baptism and confirmation, care should be taken to avoid the impression that they are identical with confirmation. In the case of people who have not been confirmed, it will be more appropriate for the incumbent to propose that they be confirmed.

Comment

While these guidelines may be regarded as a breakthrough, they need to be treated with great care. The bishop can still prevent children receiving communion prior to confirmation in his diocese, and PCC or incumbent can prevent it in the parish. Parents can prevent their baptized children receiving the sacrament. There is no right of the baptized child here, only the possibility of permission.

Secondly, the language of 'understanding' is at best vague. No age limit is set: Guidelines talk of an 'appreciation of the significance of the sacrament' (d), deliberately avoiding words like 'understanding' or 'discernment,' but *preparation* is required, and paragraph (e) with regard to those with learning difficulties, does expect *discernment*. The tone is of allowing the admission of children of school-going age, but the theology is most unclear, and the whole smacks more of tolerating an anomaly, than of leading the church in new insights.

Thirdly, confirmation remains solidly in place as a necessary rite. The final sentences of paragraphs (b) and (j) make this very clear. What confirmation might mean is not made clear, though the new liturgies in 'Common Worship' do give some idea. It is, sadly,outside the scope of this booklet to pursue this important question. I just hope that the cart of confirmation will not drive the horses of baptism and communion.

Paragraph (i) recognizes the problem that arises when children have been in separate groups for the first or main part of the service. It is not appropriate for children to rush in and straight to the rail—as often happens for the blessing. The guidelines stipulate the presence of the children for the Eucharistic Prayer, but it is worth asking whether there might not be an option for a children's group leader praying with the children, including in the prayer the mention that the bread and wine have been blessed, and preparing them for receiving. Some in our church have raised the issue of absolution if the children are 'out' for the prayers of penitence. Should the children not be absolved before receiving communion?

The most positive note is struck in paragraph (j) where a child once admitted cannot be excluded in another parish, while remaining in good standing with the church. Yet this paragraph is also the most tendentious: it is the only paragraph where the right of the child is able to overrule the parish or diocese. It is the only Guideline that will allow variant practice against the will of the bishop or parish. The final sentences seem to imply that the new incumbent might want to see the child confirmed as soon as possible to regularize matters. There remains the obvious pastoral problem (though not a new one) where a family with two or more children move to a new parish where children are not admitted. The older child may have been admitted at 7 in the first church; the younger may have to wait many years. Reducing the age for confirmation may be an immediate pastoral solution, but it is not good practice.

It may seem churlish to be so unenthusiastic about positive changes, but these guidelines are pastoral softening, not theological changes. Despite the fact that the Anglican Communion and the Church of England have accepted that Christian initiation is complete in baptism, still the young baptized are denied their new birthright, and any age guideline provided in a diocese may quickly become a new orthodoxy, a new limit, though it is hard to see how it will ever be justified for long. Some bishops are making it difficult for parishes to move forward; each bishop can add further guidelines and rules for his diocese. It seems we have not moved further than Jeremy Taylor's view of the seventeenth century, where the admission of children, while it may be right, should be withheld for ecclesial expediency.

However, these guidelines are now in the public sphere and can be used to help parishes move forward. Some of the practical implications will be addressed in the next chapter.

- How might these Guidelines affect your parish?
- Do you know what is the view of your bishop, what else your diocese might require, whom to contact, and how to proceed?

5

Practical Issues with Regard to Admitting Children to Communion

Initiating the Process

1. *Gauge the depth of feeling on this subject.* While there are general theological principles involved there is also a congregation, made up of individuals and families, with other groupings, each with their own investment in this subject, or in its implications for them. For many this is a disturbing and dangerously innovative procedure, and one they are not too happy with. Different traditions have different emphases on 'understanding' and/or ritual. It is vital to know how best to raise the subject, how to air it and how to help the PCC and congregation come to a decision. Above all, leave enough quality time to discuss it, and then time to reflect. Do not hurry through the debate, or hurry to vote; take time to explain and for digestion to take place. Indeed, the bishop may well want to see evidence of this.

2. *Ministers will need to try and preempt obvious blocking tactics, and rein in the over-exuberant.* Remember it is easier to block something and prevent it than to bring into being and to create. Ask a neighbouring church where children do receive communion to send representatives to a PCC meeting, both ordained and lay (parents of young children are good advocates). Ask members of the PCC to go to a church where children do receive communion to see what it is like. Talk to individuals beforehand. Know your facts, and use them graciously. It is worth pointing out that this is already

Anglican practice in some parts of the world (New Zealand, South Africa, Canada and USA) and Methodist practice, at least in many churches. It is not stepping off the known world.

3. *Know the eucharistic nature of your church.* What is the local understanding of communion? What changes have been introduced recently and what has been blocked? How are children already incorporated? Who is wanting change? Can you envisage what particular changes might mean in reality in your church? How will it fit into other plans? A course on the meaning and history of communion may be a worthwhile consideration.

4. *Know what your own diocesan procedures are, and who to contact.* Do not attempt on your own what could be supported by others. Many traditionally-minded people will be swayed (somewhat) by diocesan support. So use it! Know too, if your bishop has any hang-ups on the subject. Be prepared!

Instructing the Children

Guideline (d) requires an 'appropriate and serious pattern of preparation,' but what this means is not stipulated. It is up to the church to consider how much the child should be taught before receiving communion, and how much they should know. How much should be in a specific and extra programme— and that can make communion more special, especially if love and effort is put in by leaders—and how much should simply be the ongoing instruction and teaching of the children as part of their Sunday attendance (and this assumes a reasonable regularity of attendance) is for the church to decide, though there may be diocesan guidelines here.

There are numerous resources now available. Choose a course that seems appropriate for your church, and reflects what you feel the children need to know, and is an appropriate length. Depending on the length and style, you will need to work out when best to do the preparation. Afternoons after school may work but children can be tired and have other things on. Saturday morning is a good time for some, but bad for many. If the instruction takes place in the 'Sunday School' time, then this prevents the need for further meetings as well as the feeling that communion is a reward for completing a course. It may however not be practicable, due to lack of space or lack of teachers (if not all the group are being instructed), and it may not give enough time for certain courses. The more entertaining and friendly the instruction is, the better. Food and fun mixed in will make it a pleasure not a chore.

It is certainly a good idea to let the children taste the bread/wafers and the wine as early as possible to demystify the elements and so they can concentrate on what they mean. Likewise it is good to have at least one session in the church around the table explaining the general mechanics and the specific choreography for their first communion.

It is very important that parents or guardians are kept fully informed and are as involved as possible in the process. You will need to send a letter to parents first. Whatever programme is developed, make sure that the first meeting is with parents present, and aim to get the children to take work home to do with parents so as to involve them in the instruction. Good communication is important.[20]

It is as important to educate the congregation. Particularly the first time, they too need instruction. You may wish to ask for sponsors for the children; it may be good to put their photos on a display, their names on a news-sheet, and to pray for them regularly through the course.

Initiating the Children

The Guidelines require a register to be kept, and the 'occasion…marked in some suitable way before the whole congregation' (f). They do not say how this is to be done, but Guideline (l) says it should not be a quasi-confirmation. The Knaresborough Report deliberately decided against marking this moment, on the grounds that it should not become a further initiation point. In a South African church we know there is no joint preparation, no act of initiation. As parents or children request it, so the minister talks to the family together, and then the child is welcome, and is expected to be in the church for the eucharistic prayer. The other children in the church come in at the end of communion and receive a blessing, as happens in many churches here. Here there are now texts in preparation (for commendation by the House of Bishops) to mark the admission of children; they do not contain any responses for the children. Others however feel a response of some kind is important, but it is difficult to know quite what the children need to affirm. Behind this is the whole question of sufficient discernment and understanding, tackled in chapter 3.

If a level of understanding is expected, not only are those with learning difficulties potentially excluded, but the event is being marked as another milestone on the journey not necessarily of faith but of understanding and knowledge. If there is no explicit understanding or response required then can one justify excluding the younger ones? It may therefore be better to mark the occasion by the involvement of the children in the service, with a celebration afterwards, but with the minister explaining and declaring. Might one start along these lines: 'Today we welcome x, y and z as communicant members of the church. They have learnt together how special the communion is. As they continue as members of God's family with us, we share in their joy, and ask God's continued blessing upon them…'

There is a tension in this, especially for those who would prefer to include infants from baptism. To mark admission in a major way is to seem to make

---

20 There may be difficulties if the child comes to church without parents. Obviously their permission must be sought, and a sponsor from the church may be appointed to help. If done sensitively this should not be a major problem in most cases.

communion dependent on some further instruction, a theologically mistake. But not to mark it may be to disadvantage not just those children for whom this is their point of admission, but also their younger siblings who want to know why they are excluded. A special service helps this pastorally.

How can the children be included on this special Sunday? There are several ways to include them. They can have chosen the songs and hymns and help with readings and/or prayers; they can make up the offertory party, and receive communion first with their families or sponsors. Some churches give certificates and gifts—a Bible perhaps—and some choose a special Sunday, Pentecost, or a guest preacher. There can be a church party afterwards. Inclusion in the service is probably more appropriate than mere inclusion in the text.

It is also worth thinking what age might be appropriate, and what time of year—Pentecost has good theological basis, and the previous weeks being school time might be good for preparation, though half-term is often awkward. September is a time when children change school year and might be good for that reason, though prior preparation is hard during summer holidays. At our church, having tried Pentecost, we now plan to try out an October admission date.

Involving the Children at the Communion

Have we given children early entrance to an adult rite, used the 12 or PG warning somewhat irresponsibly, or will we also change the film in the cinema to a U? Here we will consider some immediate issues, and in the next chapter consider some of the implications of recognizing that children are equally welcome at the Lord's table.

Children nowadays are not educated in rows facing the front, receiving knowledge; education is more interactive and busy. In church the children have often been active and interactive in their small groups for the first part of the service. They can find the passivity of the eucharistic celebration very trying. Adults who see this prayer as the culmination of the service, can find children more than a distraction. However there are ways of including children in a fairly traditional service.

Children can be involved as servers and with the offertory; they can be brought to stand around the table. (They can be left to hang around at the edges of church, as teenagers like to do, left to their own devices until they come to the rail. Not all want to be involved after all). Children can be asked to lead the acclamation of faith, to say the post-communion sentence or lead into the prayer.

Younger children are most easily involved if there are easy words or easy songs. A sung Lord's Prayer with a complex setting will exclude them; if it is said, they can join in at this point at least. Will we 'sacrifice' the sung setting for the children? At least on occasion? Might the children not sing at this point too, in place of the Agnus Dei?

Children are also best coming to the rail early rather than later since their concentration will more easily wander; families may be encouraged to sit nearer the front where they can see better and receive communion first. (Obviously some will prefer to be to the edge or the back in case children are felt to be too unruly.) In some churches the children could then help the choir sing as others receive communion.

At times children will be somewhat self-conscious, sometimes apparently irreverent, but then maybe they do not hide their real thoughts as well as adults! That said, we have not had a single incident in five years of a child misbehaving badly while receiving communion.

The way children are involved will inevitably depend on how many children are present, how large the congregation is, how formal the service, and what space is available. It should be a matter for discussion—adult worshippers should not begrudge them some space and opinion. As an issue it should be considered, practically, along with issues like disabled access, and user-friendliness, to give but two other examples. What we are willing to do will depend on the priority given to the issue, and the limits within the particular building and congregation. Space for eight wheelchairs may be needed in some churches, not (yet) in others. Making space, even for one, may be costly. We may expect everyone whoever they are to behave as we do; we may be willing to adapt. A listed building with a high altar, little chancel space and fixed oak pews will be more difficult to change spatially than a church hall.

How long does it take a church to change a light bulb? It may depend on the diocesan office and a faculty but more likely the answer is: 'As long as it takes them really to want to change it.'

- How much do we want the involvement of children *as children?*
- Do we see them as people in their own right, or do we want them to behave as little adults?
- How could you involve the children in your church better?

6
Implications: Can we Face them?

Eucharistic Language and Liturgy

In a survey of the Anglican churches of our deanery every minister agreed that the current eucharistic prayers are inappropriate with children present; the language, the structure, the length and the imagery are all in need of change, but not just because they are not child-friendly—they are not even congregation-friendly! The new prayers being considered do not seem much different in tone, though Prayers D and E are probably the best to use with children present. Others obviously treasure the traditional liturgy. Changing words on its own will not make for 'better' services. Liturgy is more than simply a set of words. Anglican ministers have a set liturgy which they may dream away but it remains a reality with which they must work. Hopefully the recognition that children are full members of the eucharistic fellowship may help liturgists move to a less cerebral style of worship in due time.

Ritual and Practice

Just as language and words need reconsidering for their accessibility so our ritual, our actions and practices need assessing. Just because something has been done one way for years is not a reason either for changing it or for retaining it. In most Anglican churches the practice has changed hugely over the centuries and many older buildings will testify to that. Few if any of us really believe that an altar rail is of the *esse* of communion, nor do we know why we kneel or stand to receive, nor the ferocious arguments through history on the subject!

All of us have adapted our lifestyles through life. Few of us would put up with unwanted or cumbersome furniture in our house, except for a very good reason, but we can be tragically museum-minded with our churches.

But there may be no need to change ritual or practice, or only little things. Nobody is suggesting turning every church into a crèche facility. As we try to make space (physical and other) for adults so we should do the same for the children too—make room for all. Children, just like adults, will vary between whether they like lots of variety or not; they will want freshness and security of pattern; non-readers will want common texts they can join in. Children are not going to wreck the Church of England as we know it!

The Place of Confirmation

This is a huge subject, and is as much to do with our Anglican heritage, teenage psychology, and our understanding of rites of passage, as it is to do with children receiving communion. There are some who are saying 'confirm at 7 and have done' which is no answer. It is outside the scope of this booklet to find answers. Suffice it to say that (with respect to theology) few people now claim that confirmation is either a part of Christian initiation, or a prerequisite for receiving communion; with respect to sociology, we need to recognize the movement into an adult faith and adult membership of a group (the church). Practically, given people now come to faith at all and any ages, any ritual of self-affirmation of faith (as distinct from a parental desire for the child) will necessarily have to be able to encompass people of vastly varied background and age. We need some such rite for a public affirmation of faith and confirmation of belonging. The new *Initiation Services* go some way to meeting these points.

7

The Importance of the Issue of Children and Communion

Most churches have their own tensions and difficulties as well as their strengths and joys. Many are struggling to cope with all the changes going on, whether the joining together of parishes, loss of numbers, ordination of women, use of buildings or whatever. The admittance of children to communion prior to confirmation is a contentious issue in some churches, and one that the minister may feel is not a priority. There are more important battles to fight.

At one level this may be true. There may be few children in the church, and they may be accommodated with a blessing. But to the extent that it makes us consider the deeper meaning of communion, who it is for, and on what grounds, then this becomes a major issue at the heart of our worshipping identity. The admittance of children to communion was the *first* article of 23 at the Synod of St Wenceslas in 1418, central because it emphasized that the sacrament was truly for all the baptized.[21] It is unlikely to be the first article of modern day churches, but where then on the list?

- What are the battlefields in your church—open, rumbling, or latent?
- Over what sort of issues are they fought?
- Is the exclusion of baptized members from communion not a serious problem? (If it was not children but an adult group that was excluded, might we not make more of a fuss?)

---

21 See Holeton, *Infant Communion—Then and Now*, p 11.

Because this is to do with the sacrament it is not a peripheral issue, though in some churches there may be more urgent issues to attend to. Because it is to do with the heart of our worship—especially for the more catholic churches—it is an issue that needs dealing with very sensitively.

And there is a final question to ask: For whom are we doing this? Hopefully we are changing because we recognize the children who are members of the family should be fully included. Hopefully we are changing because we believe it to be a right move. But, hopefully, we are also doing it within the context of the mission of the church. In itself, admitting the baptized child to communion could be no more than reordering our internal worship. In fact, the effort expended in making the change could, if we are not careful, while strengthening our eucharistic worship, actually diminish our mission and outreach. There is always the danger of becoming a eucharistic sect, where our sense of belonging is gained at the expense of excluding others. I have already noted that the sacraments can be both a sign of inclusion and a sign of exclusion. As a church, we need to ask:

- How will the inclusion of our children strengthen the mission of our church?
- How do we spot signs of becoming too inward focused, a eucharistic sect?
- How can we resist and combat such tendencies?

A church where every member, whether young or old, is seen to be united in the grace of God, can be a challenge and a witness to its community, distinctive, attractive and welcoming. Each church must make its own journey, its own changes. God's Spirit, local tensions and modern culture and ideas will mould, remould and resist moulding in unique ways. Our prayer must be that our worship is renewed, to the greater glory of God and for the proclamation of his grace and glory in our world. To worship in Spirit and in truth requires a careful and deep consideration of who is welcome at the Lord's table. May this booklet help a little in that reflection.